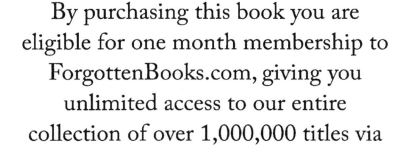

ISBN 978-0-483-05038-9
PIBN 10126852

AN ORATION,

DELIVERED AT THE ENCŒNIA

OF THE

UNIVERSITY OF NEW BRUNSWICK,

FREDERICTON, N. B.,

25th June, 1868,

BY THE

Hon. JOHN HAMILTON GRAY, D. C. L., Q. C., M. P.,

ALUMNI ORATOR FOR 1868.

[PUBLISHED BY REQUEST.]

SAINT JOHN, N. B.
PRINTED BY BARNES AND COMPANY,
PRINCE WILLIAM STREET.
1868.

ORATION.

MR. PRESIDENT
and Alumni of the University:

THOUGH I can claim no lineage, if such an expression may
be permitted, with your Institution, yet I may truly say
that ever since entering on public life I have taken a deep
interest in its welfare. Eighteen years ago, on first beco-
ming a member of the Assembly of this Province, I found the
College assailed by some of the public men of the day with
a bitterness which it is now difficult to realize : it was saved,
but for seven long years it was nurtured in convulsion.
The vigorous tree, which now gathers beneath its broad
spreading branches many happy hearts, drawing vitality
and strength from its precious fruits, was then torn and
rent by many a ruthless hand. Dark and cheerless were
its prospects : the withering blast and the blinding storm
bore down upon it, but its roots were deep and strong : it
withstood the tempest, and it now stands forth regenerated
and revived. It is well that the trials of this Institution
should be known to you. The greatest benefits a country
possesses are sometimes jeopardized by those professedly
acting in its interests—some from ignorance, some from
causes or motives even less creditable.

The early management of this Institution, under its
original Charter as King's College, is known not to have
given satisfaction. It was complained, and justly, that
the large annual subsidy from the public purse for its support produced no corresponding benefit ; and it was pro-
posed in the Legislature that that subsidy should be
withdrawn, and the amount divided among other Institutions, or devoted to other public purposes. The intensity

of feeling which characterized those discussions may be
gathered from the public journals and debates of the Assembly from 1852 to 1860; but it will startle the Alumni
to hear that it was at that time gravely laid down by a
member of the Legislature, then high in the political circles
of the day, that a superior education, or such as could be
obtained at College, was quite unnecessary in New Brunswick—that in the history of the Province, the men who
had got on the best were men of no education—and that,
therefore, for all practical purposes, Institutions of the
character of this University were not required, and their
support from the public purse was consequently an im-
proper waste of the public funds. In vain, at first, was it
pointed out that the mismanagement of an Institution
ought not to affect the principle involved in the main-
tenance and encouragement of superior education; that
while it was the duty of the Legislature to reform the Institution, it was still more their imperative duty not to
permit its mismanagement to operate to the sacrifice of the
principle. The strenuous efforts of its friends at length
prevailed, and in 1854, under an Act of the Legislature
passed for the purpose, a Commission was appointed to
" enquire into the (then) state of King's College, its
" management and utility, with a view of improving the
" same, and rendering the Institution more generally useful,
" and of suggesting the best mode of effecting that desirable
" object; and should such Commission deem a suspension of
" the Charter desirable, then to suggest the best mode of
" applying the endowment, in the mean time, for the edu-
" cational purposes of the Province."
It is due to Sir Edmund Head, then the Lieutenant Go-
vernor of this Province—a most accomplished scholar and
an untiring friend of education—to say that he took the
warmest interest in maintaining the College, and in bring-
ing about that reform which would make it acceptable to
the people; and that by his suggestion Dr. Ryerson of To-
ronto, and Mr. Dawson, then of Nova Scotia—at present

the President of the McGill College at Montreal—were placed upon the Commission. The Hon. Mr. Saunders, Mr. James Brown, of Charlotte County, and myself were the remaining members of the Commission. In the session of 1855 the Commissioners made their report; and it is under the system recommended in that report, and which was after some years further discussion in the Legislature substantially adopted, that the University is now so successfully conducted. To Dr. Ryerson the Commissioners were particularly indebted, and it is but due to the present President and Professors to say that to their cordial co-operation and judicious management that success is mainly to be attributed. The character of the Institution was entirely changed. From a College, limited to one denomination and disliked by all others—because supported from the funds of all—it became a University covering with its broad ægis all the educational establishments of the country. It takes by the hand the infant child in the Parish school, and points to him that County scholarship which his industry may attain. It tells the struggling parent, whose scant means might bid him turn away, that his country will provide for the expanding intellect of his child. It tells the young scholar within its walls who thirsts for knowledge, that the fountains which can supply him are at his command ; that in the practical sciences of chemistry, geology, mechanics, astronomy, as applicable to civil engineering, surveying, agriculture, commerce or navigation—all that will be useful to him to learn—he can have. To those who desire to try the classic walks of Greece and Rome, to study the records of the great Past, to learn how nations rose and fell, the University affords every opportunity ; and to those who wish to become acquainted with modern languages and literature, equal facilities are extended.

But above all, it establishes the broad fact that within your own country and under your own institutions can be found the means of enabling you to take your place amid the foremost men of the world, by the attainment of the highest education at home. If there is one thing, more than another which tends to foster an attachment to one's own country—to bring back in after years and when wandering in foreign climes the longing wish for home, the pride of one's native land—it is the recollection of one's school boy days. Why is it that an Eton boy is always an Eton boy, whether amid the defiles of Abyssinia or on the burning plains of India? Why is it that an Englishman is so terribly English (if such an expression may be excused), be he where he may? It is because his thoughts are associated with all those early scenes where first his youthful sports were held—where his cricketing, his boating, his hunting, his shooting, his fishing, his boxing, were first enjoyed— where his very larks were run; yet where at the same time he was storing his mind with that learning which was to be the working material of his after life—where he was daily hearing the institutions of his country, her laws, her very faults discussed—where week by week he learns of some great name, or some heroic achievement, or some illustrious statesman adding new blazonry to his country's scroll of fame; and so in time his patriotism becomes intensified, and it makes no difference whether she be right or wrong, he stands by his country — and so he ought. When your young men are sent away to foreign lands for education, they are very apt to become more attached to the associations where they are than to those they have left. The impressions first made on the youthful mind are the most lasting, and it is the duty of every parent in New Brunswick to educate, if he can, his children at his own University before sending them abroad, if he desires that in after life those children should be devoted to her interests.

It is on account of the broad principles that are laid down in this report, and of their successful application, that I call it to your attention; but as it covers more than a mere reference to this University—as it takes up the whole question of education in New Brunswick, from the common schools upwards—as it advocates direct taxation for schools and the establishment of a Normal school on an enlarged scale, I may be excused in quoting some observations by Dr. Wayland (addressed to myself as Chairman of the Commission), after perusing it. Dr. Wayland was regarded as the first *educationist* in the United States, had been the reformer of the Brown University in Rhode Island, and had, at great length, and with great kindness, explained to the Commissioners his views, on their visiting him at Providence.

It is to be borne in mind, in considering these observations, that New Brunswick was peculiarly situated in having the power to adopt these principles and changes without any interference with vested rights. Eminent writers in England strongly advocate them, but the Universities of Oxford and Cambridge were founded long before religious equality was recognized, and on their foundation, privileges and rights were conceded which it is difficult now to assail. Equally so was it with the University at Cambridge, in Massachusetts; though how far those rights are regarded at present, I am not prepared to say.

Dr. Wayland says:—"I have read the Report of the "Commission with attention. You will allow me to exclude "from my remarks the kind allusion which you have made "to my poor services. I have labored long, I hope from "public motives, and with small results. This is all I can "claim—all the rest is owing to your kind partiality.

"As to the Report itself, I hardly know how to express "my gratitude and satisfaction. As a man, I return to you "my deep felt thankfulness for the generous spirit of en-"lightened Christian humanity which it breathes in every "sentence. It knows of no party, of no sect, of no rank, "but in an all-embracing public spirit encircles the whole "people of New Brunswick, providing for every individual "the education which he needs, and enabling every one to "carry this education as far and in precisely the direction "he wishes. It moreover takes especial care of the common "schools, making every arrangement under them as perfect

" as possible, and to carry this improved education within
" the reach of every man. · Should this Bill pass, and· its
" provisions be thoroughly carried out, it will be the greatest
" boon that has· ever been conferred on any people. Others
" have, I doubt not, meant as well ; but they have not en-
" joyed the light that has shone on you from all preceding
" experiments; and in no case that I have seen has the best
" good of *the whole people* been so thoroughly considered.
" Besides, your education is to be a Christian education,
" while it most carefully abstains from interfering with the
" religious convictions of any sect whatever. It seems to me
" that your whole people must pass it by acclamation. And
" I must add that I firmly believe that to whatever attain-
" ment in virtue and wealth, in arts and civilization, New
" Brunswick may arrive, after generations will look back
" upon this Act as the starting point from which her pro-
" gress commenced and the source from which all her bles-
" sings flowed. This, however, cannot be accomplished in a
" day.   It will take some time to organize your schools ; it
" will take time to prepare for them competent teachers ; it
" will take time for these scholars, thus taught, to advance
" far enough to enter your higher schools. It may take some
" time to convince men of the reality of the blessings you
" offer them. Men are so much accustomed to heartless
" legislation that they are slow to believe that a plan of this
" kind is really intended for their good ; and besides, the
" flourishing condition of the Province itself presents obsta-
" cles. Where land can be obtained at so low a rate, where
" taxes are so low, and the opportunities of securing a com-
" petence or abundance are so frequent, some are prone to
" undervalue education. We find this the case in the United
" States, and this constitutes the great difference between us
" and Europe ; but all these difficulties will be removed by
" time.   In due season you will reap if you faint not; and
" you will have the privilege of inscribing your names on
" the list of those who have conferred inestimable blessings
" on humanity."

The opinion of Dr. Wayland on this system is, of itself, sufficient authority for its adoption.

We have, then, this starting point, that at home you have an Institution capable of affording to your young men, at a very moderate expense, the highest elements of education, a practical useful education, or a refined intellectual education, or both combined. Let us look back for a moment. A century has not rolled by since on the spot where we now stand the wild Indian had his home. Centuries had followed upon centuries, and son succeeded sire, without change. The winter's cold and the summer's heat came in their turn, and nature bloomed and withered as the vernal sun or autumn's blasts gave or destroyed life. The River rolled on its mighty volume to the sea, and rose and fell as it does now with the melting snows or the parching droughts; but its banks gave no sign of advancing civilization. What had been, was—'twas still the same. Yet in all that constitutes a man the Indian was as perfect as ourselves—as lithe of frame, as subtle of intellect, as keen in the pursuit of pleasure, as enduring, as courageous, more temperate, more chaste, in council as wise, in war as daring. Look now along the banks of this same River. Towns and villages, and cities, and farms, and institutions of learning, and trade and commerce,—all speak of an advancing and permanent civilization, tending to promote the happiness and elevation of your race; and the chimes of your Christian churches, as on the Sabbath eve they echo from your hills and are borne along your valleys and your plains, speak of a civilization whose benefits are not to be limited by time. Whence, then, this change? What makes this difference? Need I say it simply results from that education of which you have the opportunity of availing yourselves—from that education which, since the discovery of printing, has enabled our forefathers and ourselves to start with all the advantages of a knowledge of the Past, and to draw from the storehouses of the Dead the means of sustaining and extending the material progress of the living. I have told you that it was said on the floors of the Assembly, that a superior education was of no advantage in New Brunswick. Let us try it out. The rude bar of iron in its raw state is a powerful weapon. It crushes and mangles, and in the hands of a strong man may be made subservient to the worst or best of purposes ; but when moulded and welded and refined into the polished steel, does it lose its strength, or is it less dangerous or less useful when, directed by the same powerful hand, it flashes as the falchion's blade, or drives the great steam engine to its work? So with the strong intellect : it does not lose its strength because it is educated.

It is not my duty, as it certainly is not my intention, to enter into a disquisition of the best systems of Education, or the mode by which you will acquire the greatest amount of useful information. That emphatically falls within the purview of those who are professors and tutors in the College. I care not to reason with you as to the best rendering of a Latin translation, or to be hypercritical about a Greek derivation; I prefer to address you as men who, in a few short years, will have to take your part in the *onward* destinies of your country—whose minds for weal or woe will make their impress on the events of the coming day, and to remind you that as those minds are liberally stored and well expanded, so in proportion will be the greatness, the happiness, and the prosperity of your native land. It is necessary that you should look beyond the small circle in which you move—that you should realize the fact that no limited coterie constitutes the sole motive power of the causes which bring about great events. Study the constitutional and parliamentary histories of England, France and the United States. In those three countries the great principles of constitutional freedom and commercial progress have been best developed. What Burke and Webster said, what Mirabeau proclaimed, what Hamilton wrote, what May collates, make the subject of

earnest consideration : and depend upon it, when you take
your part in the active affairs of life, your conclusions will
be founded upon the suggestions of the ablest minds, and
your actions determined by the experience of men who
thought not merely, but tested the correctness of their
thoughts by great measures, tending to elevate their several
countries in the scale of nations.

The preparation for a statesman's career is of more im-
portance to you now than it has hitherto been. The mere
book learning of a College, however great it be, will not
alone avail you in the struggle of life. To lead men—to
guide men, you must know the human heart—the causes
and the springs of action. The philosophy of history is a
study apart from a mere knowledge of the events of history. The forms of government—their permanence—
their results upon the amelioration of the people—their
tendency to preserve law and order—from the days of the
Republics of Greece and Rome down to the present time,
are matters with which you must make yourselves familiar.
The great code of the Civil Law from the Pandects of Jus-
tinian down to that still greater Common Law of England,
on which now rest the liberties of half the world, must equally
form the subject of your study. The relative rights of the
Baron and the Serf—the fiefs of the Feudal times—have
passed away before the advancing spirit of the age ; but
their very terms are interwoven in our daily language,
and their theories are at the foundation of our dearest rights.
How can you deal with the Future, if you are entirely ignorant of the Past? How are you prepared to say which
government is best, if you really have no knowledge of
any? How can you undertake to legislate to remedy an
evil, if you do not know what is the root of the wrong?
These are not the subjects which ordinarily come within
the scope of a Collegiate course ; but you must make them
your supplementary subjects, if you wish to be statesmen.

You must feel that in the broader career which is now
being opened to the young men of New Brunswick, the

days of ignorance have been numbered; and the representative whose mind is a "tabula rasa," must stand with an " orê clausô. He is powerless to do his countrymen any good; and he lessens them in the estimation of strangers, because he is assumed to be a fair specimen of his race. I implore you then, as you regard the honor of your country, to make good use of the opportunities you now have at this University. But why, it may be said, is there greater reason for this preparation as statesmen now than before? Have we not seen men in our own Assembly who could not speak or write ten words of English correctly—who could not tell you whether William the Norman was the last of the Barons or the first of the Guelphs, and would hesitate to decide whether Rome was in Greece or Athens in Italy—who knew nothing of Governments or Constitutions, or Parliaments or precedents—have we not seen such men holding the highest positions, and sitting in the Councils of the country? *True, you have. But the times have changed.* This very University, during the last eight years, has sent forth into the country a number of intelligent young men who are already making their mark. The other institutions of learning have also done the same. This very day more are going out.* Education is being more generally diffused and more appreciated. Your competitors will be more able and more numerous. ·But above and beyond this, our Provincial position has changed. We are no longer members of the scattered sections of a wide domain—we are no longer isolated in our interests or our powers—we are no longer the sole arbiters of our own Fate. Our actions hereafter influence not ourselves alone, but others. Let us look at that position calmly, in reference to the new duties which devolve upon us. Let us look at it under the stern aspect of reality,—not *as to what we would or should have done, or left undone,*—not as to what prejudice would dictate, or what enthusiasm would suggest.

---

* Twelve Students graduated this day.

.Let us look at it as a matter unchangeable—*for it will not be changed*—and let us urge our young men, in their studies at this University, to prepare themselves to go on and win the first prizes of the Dominion, and by their abilities and character to extend the power and the influence of their Province.

Knowledge is Power. In Science—in Trade—in War—in Peace—in movements by land or by water, in all that pertains to the influence, the improvement, the happiness, the progress of men or nations—Knowledge is Power.

Our first knowledge should be a thorough acquaintance with the extent, character and resources of our own country—not simply of those parts of which it is now constituted, but of those other parts which, within a few short years, will be embraced within its limits, and which will bring under one control the vast domains of British North America, spreading from the Atlantic to the Pacific—domains teeming with exhaustless wealth, and waiting but our enterprise and energy to become the happy homes of many of our countrymen.

Of Nova Scotia, of New Brunswick, of old Canada, we have many authentic records; and all are familiar with their previous histories; but I will for a few moments invite the attention of the Alumni to other lands less known—to those lands beyond Lake Superior, for which it will be their lot, in a few years, to legislate.

In the history of the world civilization seems to have started from the East—its tendency has been towards the West. The civilization of a large portion of the West is yet to come—that of the East seems to be, of, the past. As far back as our authentic records go, the plains of Asia have teemed with busy and industrious populations, advanced in the elements of science and the practice of pursuits which tend to make great cities, produce great works, and give an apparently permanent character to the Institutions under which their people lived. If we permit ourselves to believe records which, with reference to our own,

B

may almost be termed pre-historic—in China, for instance, there was a civilization in the far East, complete and systematic, which the great body of mankind at the present day little realize or comprehend, yet the evidences of that civilization are to be found. Amid the jungles of Cambodia and Siam are the ruins of temples of vast proportions and elaborate structure—with lofty corridors of magnificent columns, whose massive pedestals and sculptured capitals indicate not only a dense population—a bygone population—but a population advanced in refinement and architectural knowledge. But what history tells who those people were, or when they lived? The tiger roams through the sculptured halls; the civilization is effete; no mental power characterises the people of those lands. In the family of nations they hold the lowest place, and the strong hand of European power crumples them to its will as ambition or policy dictates.

There is not a man in this crowded Hall, who can call back the teaching of his school thirty years ago, who was not taught that the great interior of Africa was a barren waste—a sandy desert, where no life, no vegetation thrived. Yet what do we now learn? That it abounds with magnificent plains of great verdure; with noble rivers and lakes; with lofty mountains, whose summits, covered with perpetual snow, supply an unceasing irrigation; that its table lands are clothed with dense forests; that tropical fruits and cereals abound. Knowledge is power. The happiness of millions may yet depend upon that knowledge. The civilization of the East, engrafted on the sterner characteristics of the European races, moved Westward over to America; but even there, in some parts, the existence of a prior civilization was found. In Mexico and Peru the organization of strong and powerful governments secured the happiness and well-being of thriving and populous nations, rivalling those of the East in numbers and advancement. Temples were there of solid build, and even three centuries of ruthless modern occupation have not obliterated the traces of former greatness. But in the interior of British North America—in the far North West, are great regions of undeveloped wealth; where no prior civilization has placed its mark; where no ruined monuments tell of bygone times; where nature alone remains the undisputed master of the broad domain; where seasons follow seasons rich with all their varied beauties, and rivers and inland seas rise and fall untrammelled by the hand of man.

This country of undeveloped wealth, where there is no effete civilization to revive—whose history is to be written in the future—where every niche in the Temple of Fame is yet unoccupied—this country of vast extent it will be for you, in a short time, to bring into States, and Territories, and reduce into organized governments. You will find, when you have studied the subject, that it is a country of wonderful fertility, of a climate exactly similar to that of Fredericton; that its very seasons are the same, and that in consequence of the peculiar formation of the great American Desert, which commences about 98° of west longitude, extending westwardly to the base of the Rocky Mountains, and northwardly almost from Texas to the 49th parallel of latitude, or our boundary—the only passage to the Pacific through a fertile region, and in a salubrious climate, lies within our Territory—and through our Territory the great North West Road must pass. The Americans would gladly have this Territory, and willingly pay for it enough to wipe away the whole debt of the Dominion. But this must not be. A nation's fate is trembling in the scale, and our own young men must be the founders of our Western Empire. We cannot give up our own flag and our own nationality, and the traditions of a thousand years, and the Sovereign we revere, and the Institutions under which we are free. We must extend to this Territory the blessings we enjoy, and you must prepare yourselves, by your present studies—by your present industry —to be the wise Statesmen and Legislators through whose means these results shall be achieved.

An American poet (George Whittier) has so beautifully expressed the future of the West that, with the alteration of a single verse to make it applicable to ourselves, I shall take the liberty of quoting his words :—

> "I hear the tread of Pioneers,
>   Of nations yet to be,
> The first low wash of waves, where soon
>   Shall roll a human sea.
>
> "The rudiments of Empire here
>   Are plastic yet, and warm,
> The chaos of a mighty world
>   Is rounding into form.
>
> "Each rude and jostling fragment soon
>   Its fitting place shall find ;
> The raw materials of a State,
>   Its muscle and its mind.
>
> "And westering still, the star which leads
>   The new world in its train,—
> Has tipped with fire the icy spears
>   Of many a mountain chain.
>
> "Young Columbia's snowy cones,
>   Are kindling on its way,
> And long Saskatchawan's golden sands,
>   Gleam brighter in its ray.
>
> "I hear the tread of Pioneers,
>   Of nations yet to be,
> The first low wash of waves, where soon
>   Shall roll a human sea."

But this great West will only be a part of the scene of your labors. You have not only to develope the resources of a part, but of the whole country. You have to consolidate a people ; you have to merge the jealousies of existing sections, and bind them by a common interest to each other—not to regard a commercial Tariff or a particular Law as it may operate upon a part, but as it may result in a healthy benefit to the whole. If a public expenditure is to be incurred, it must be regarded from its effect upon the United Provinces, and not from its omission to pour exhaustless wealth into a particular locality or a favorite constituency.

The tendency of modern politics, both in Europe and

America, is to fuse many small communities into one large one. Russia, Prussia and Italy are daily absorbing the smaller nations that are around them; and the United States has just passed through the most gigantic war of modern times rather than have a division of her extended empire. The effect of this policy is materially to advance the progress of the human race. If the United States had not owned California and Oregon, and her Territories on the Pacific, how long would it have been before,—nay, who could have named the time when—a Railroad would have crossed the boundless wastes of the Interior of the Continent, or scaled the Rocky Mountains?

The consolidation of countries—the abolition of interior restrictions and tariffs—must increase trade and open wide fields for labor; and as trade advances, civilization advances, and all that contributes to the material and intellectual improvement of man goes on pari passu.

As the future Statesmen of the Country, considerations of this nature must force themselves upon you; and it is while you are young,—nay, while you are even yet at College,—you must prepare your minds—you must lay the foundations for this your future work. Again, the characteristics of nations and of races must be studied. New Countries gather in the surplus populations of the Old. More than one third of our countrymen in the Dominion are descendants of another race—the first great founders of Empire in that part of America over which Her Majesty now reigns. The matchless daring of Champlain—the heroic hardihood of his companions—the unfaltering courage with which, alone, they penetrated and explored then unknown regions, peopled by fierce and savage tribes—the chivalry of Montcalm—have thrown around the history of New France a romantic interest that can never fade. Their descendants still cherish their old institutions—still speak their old language; but are as loyal and true as any people in the British Empire. Can you legislate fairly for these men without knowing their language or their history?

B2

Certainly not. Then while at College make yourselves familiar with both. You have every opportunity; and the justice you ask from them, you must be prepared to give.

Something, also, must be learned of International Law —of the conflict of Laws, and of the Rights of Nations. Your extended interests entail upon you extended responsibilities, and necessitate a corresponding care in the administration of public affairs. A conflict might arise from your indiscretion. But, even were there no such risk, the study of the broader subject expands the mind, and thus materially contributes to its education.

You cannot have too broad a field for study or for action. Little countries make little men. One thing that has materially contributed to the splendid development of the United States is that their public men of all kinds,— their young men,—their very women, think there is nothing too great for their country to undertake, or for their people to achieve. The daring which this self-reliance creates is the cause of more than one half of their success.

To young men, educated at a British University and brought up under British Institutions, it need not be said there is but one form of government which it is both their duty and their interest to maintain. Nearly eighteen hundred years ago Tacitus observed :—" Nam cunctas nationes " et urbes, populus, aut primores, aut singuli, regunt ; de- " lecta ex his et consociata reipublicæ forma laudari facilius, " quam evenire—vel si evenit, haud diuturna esse potest."* A more valuable tribute to the excellence of our Constitution could not have been conceived or expressed. However broad may be the foundation, the keystone of the arch must bind the whole together. Without an efficient controlling central authority, there can be no effectual use of great national power ; and we find in countries where the Constitution does not sufficiently give that authority, that in times of emergency the authority itself is boldly

---

* Lib. 4, Chap. 33.

assumed in direct defiance of the Law and the Constitution, by those who are administering the public affairs. But there is yet another quotation I would make, and one that must be equally appreciated and acted upon; and which lays down the correct principle, that, after all, in governments, the authority is but delegated, and it must be wielded for the benefit of those from whom it is derived. This passage is from an old Puritan Poet (of the name of George Wither), and was *in part* quoted by Mr. Bright, on a late occasion, in one of his most celebrated speeches:—

> " Let not your King and Parliament in one,
> " Much less apart, mistake themselves for that
> " Which is most worthy to be thought upon,
> " Nor think they are essentially the State.
> " But let them know *there is a deeper life*
> " *Which they but represent.*
> " That there's on earth a yet auguster thing,
> " Veiled though it be, than Parliament and King."

These two quotations contain the germ of all sound constitutional government—the principle and the mode. Books may be written—systems may be promulgated—experiments may be tried—but reduce all down to a simple proposition, and in these two quotations that proposition will be found.

I do not press these observations without serious reflection. One of the objects of education is to prepare for successful operation in the practical affairs of life. Religious and moral training, it must be assumed, may well be left to parents and tutors. In America, the great mass of the public take a deeper interest in, and exert a more powerful influence upon the affairs of their country than in England. The ancient traditions of England—the great wealth of England—enable her to have a class of men who almost exclusively take charge of the public service; and it is no uncommon thing to trace the same name in one continuous line of light from generation to generation. It is not so in America, and Canada is no exception to the rule. As your influence is therefore more extended here, so it is of consequence that your preparation should be greater. Though you may not choose to become the Parliamentary leaders, yet as the moulders of public opinion, it is essential that your views should be broad and liberal. and they cannot be broad and liberal if you are ignorant, Among educated men you will often, undoubtedly, find many whose prejudices and interests override their sense; but as a general rule educated men will be found the most liberal in their own views, and the most tolerant of the views of others. And of this character will the legislation and policy of your country partake, if you who are to direct and form it, properly prepare yourselves. You must not suppose that education will ever bring about a state of superhuman excellence. Burke has said, " That the states-" man who lays the foundation of his country's greatness " in the possession of extraordinary virtues, will find its " superstructure reared in folly and extravagance." You must expect to find men as they are—with vices, with follies, and with passions. No Utopian theory will alter nature; but the higher the degree of intelligence which is found among your people, the greater will be their comfort and their happiness, and the higher their status.

There is another thing you have to bear in mind. Ambitiou, properly directed, is the highest incentive to noble deeds. Character is not made in a day; notoriety may be obtained, not character. The latter is of slow growth; but when once obtained, affords to its possessor immense power. Few men in British America have illustrated this position more than Joseph Howe and the late Thomas D'Arcy Magee. Of the former I may not speak, because he still lives; of the latter I may. There are clouds sometimes which for a period obscure the brightest day. We should judge of life by its utility, not by its passing errors. His influence in Canada was great, and the public demonstrations at his death were not more in detestation of the atrocious crime by which his life was taken, than as an acknowledgment of the great services that that life had rendered to his adopted country. He wielded a power which, had it been directed to evil, would have deluged Canada with blood—made her soil the battle-field of contending factions—and perhaps have led to her ultimate disruption from the Empire. As it was, instead of fostering the embittered elements which were at his command, his whole energies were bent to their removal; and it is not too much to say that the unamimity which now exists is greatly owing to his counsels and his exertions. But what gave him this power? What brought it about, that a man barely past the meridian of life—who had led no great army—who had guided no revolution—who had discovered no world—who had made no startling invention—should yet have received the tribute of profound respect, from the sovereign on her throne to the humblest municipality of his country—whose death should have caused an expression of universal regret? You will find it was the simple result of a good education well directed—of continued industry well applied—of noble sentiments nobly expressed—and of a broad generous philanthropy—the consequent result of all combined. His was not the meteor mind which startled by its irregular brilliancy—it was the steady burning light which gave proof of the most careful attention. Deeply versed in all the knowledge of the past, watchful of all the movements of the present, philosophical in his reflections, practical in his suggestions, cosmopolitan in his views, and careful in his preparation, it was truly said of him:—

"Nihil tetigit quod non ornavit."

As an essayist, as a political writer, as ever ready to give his services to any good cause, without reference to creed or race, he leaves a name which few will equal; and as an orator he realized, more than any one I ever heard, Homer's description of that great man, if it may be applied to one so young,

"Τοῦ καὶ ἀπὸ γλώσσης μέλιτος γλυκίων ῥέεν αὐδή."

His case has been prominently brought before you, because his success *was the result of industry.* Go and do likewise.

I have just returned from the assembled Parliament of the country—and I tell you if you want to maintain the influence of New Brunswick in the councils of the nation, you must educate your young men to be its fitting representatives. Talk of uneducated men, beside Macdonald and Howe, and Cartier and Rose, and Galt and Holton, and Dorion and Cheauveau, and Dunkin, and Chamberlin, and a host of others who might be named—men accustomed to deal with large subjects—men who are equally familiar with the languages and literature of France and England—and who, with a thorough knowledge of Constitutional History, and the principles of Trade and Commerce, can enforce their arguments by ready references to the incidents of past and modern History, and by touches of human nature not the less dangerous, because they are subtle. There are men in that Parliament, who, by means of their strong intellect or great industry, can make their mark, and advance the interests of their constituencies and their country, even without the early advantages of a good education; but those are the very men who appreciate it the most, and give their strenuous efforts to its encouragement, and who, if they were present this day, would tell you not an hour is to be lost.

In addressing you as men who are to be the future statesmen of your country, and directing your attention to studies and reflections which may prepare you for such a position, I earnestly desire that you will not understand me as lightly appreciating the classical and mathematical studies which are particularly embraced in your course. A "double first" will carry its weight anywhere; and among the first statesmen of England are found those who have thus distinguished themselves. Pitt and Mansfield, and Lyndhurst and Brougham, and Derby and Peel, and Russell and Canning, and Romilly, and D'Israeli, and others equally well known, were remarkable for their appreciation and use of the beauties of classic literature; and Gladstone, whose position at the present day as a financier

stands unrivalled, and who is admitted to be the most refined and accomplished orator in England, adds additional
lustre to his unrivalled eloquence by rich quotations from
the Latin poets.

" Hæc studia adolescentiam alunt, senectutem oblectant,
secundas res ornant, adversis perfugium ac solatium præ-
bent; delectant domi—non impediunt foris—pernoctant
nobiscum—perigrinantur—rusticantur."

Alumni of the University, I congratulate you upon the
advantages you possess. I congratulate you upon the glo-
rious future that is before you. I congratulate you upon
the rising destinies of your country. When the gallant
soldier who now presides over the affairs of New Brunswick shall have passed away—when your Professors and
Tutors in their turn have passed away—when those who
are now active in public life in a few short years shall have
also passed away—let us hope that you, drawing your
knowledge from this University, and your inspiration from
the noblest source—your country's welfare—will go forth
prepared to advocate her interests and maintain her rights
—and that when in your turn you shall have passed away,
it may be found that many of you will have left upon the
pages of her history a lofty record and a noble name.

CPSIA information can be obtained
at www.ICGtesting.com
Printed in the USA
BVHW041757301118
534322BV00030B/267/P